INTRODUCTION TO FITNESS AND EXERCISE

THE HUMAN EXCELLENCE NETWORK

NIKHIL MADUSKAR

Copyright © Nikhil Maduskar
All Rights Reserved.

TO ALL THE INDIVIDUALS WHO AIM TO MAKE A
CHANGE AND AN IMPACT IN HUMAN WELL BEING
AND MAN'S ENDEVOURS TOWARDS GROWTH AND
PROGRESS.

A.I

Contents

CHAPTER ONE

T.H.E.N

What Is T.H.E.N?

The Human Excellence Network (T.H.E.N)

Mission –

Our mission is to help mankind in achieving its true potential by providing a platform to improve health and knowledge by following a holistic approach towards life and living it.

Vision –

The vision of our organisation is to create a platform for collaborating excellence from the field of nutrition, fitness science, healthcare, computer technology, software, artificial intelligence and spirituality for promoting human excellence and progress by catering to the holistic development of the individual in the society and help our customer/member to achieve his/her true potential. When the mind, body and spirit is taken care of then the eco-system for progressive development is established.

Built for the pursuit of human excellence – an open ended platform for fitness, nutrition, medical and allied healthcare professionals to collaborate and work for the well-being of mankind and in doing so to preserve the identity and drive growth of every individual directly or indirectly associated with the platform including technology, software and A.I.

APPROACH

Knowledge – Creating awareness and imparting knowledge in order to empower the individual to achieve excellence. To create a scientific knowledge bank and promote research in the field of fitness and health sciences. To do, you must first know.

Exercise/Movement – Man is a creature of movement and the brain and the body work together to keep us healthy. The whole idea of exercise is to engage your mind, body and heart to work together efficiently and create a bodily eco system of good health reducing the scope of disease.

Nutrition – Food is the basic necessity of life and we all eat food in order to function and stay alive. We all have a set of notions laid down by our respective ancestors as to food habits and incorporating the age old believes we shall take into considerations the effects of today's world on food.

MentalWellness - If the mind is not balanced and happy then everything falls like a castle of cards. There are plenty of short term reward boosters that can create an imbalance of brain chemistry. We all go through a phase of mild depression or stress, and here we teach mindfulness.

The foundation of **The Human Excellence Network** is based on the idea of **Universal Consciousness**.

CHAPTER TWO

FITNESS INDUSTRY

Brief Introduction to the Fitness Industry

The fitness industry includes any person, company, or entity that focuses on exercise, health, and overall maintenance of the body. It may include gyms and fitness centres, personal trainers, fitness equipment companies, food and supplement companies, orthotics, clothing companies, and sporting goods companies.

The main goal of the fitness industry is to provide services and products that promote health and wellness while drawing a profit from people's participation within the industry.

A broad range of businesses, entities, and companies fall into the category of the fitness industry since the different methods by which people train for fitness has expanded over the course of decades and even centuries. Manufacturers of soaps, locker room equipment, hot tubs, saunas, and plumbing equipment may also be included as a part of the fitness industry, as many gyms and fitness centres feature locker rooms that cater to the needs of their customers.

Sporting goods are another major part of the fitness industry, as much of fitness is focused on participating in various forms of athletic activity. Just about any sport one can choose will require specific equipment, and manufacturers will fill that need.

Sport-specific clothing companies also fall under the fitness category, as they design clothing made specifically for sports. This may mean creating and designing clothing that fits the needs of a specific sport — cycling shorts, for example — or it may mean designing and manufacturing materials that are suitable for clothing that can be used for any sport. Moisture-wicking materials are an example of such clothing.

Advertising is a key component of the industry, as all companies need a way to expose their products to potential consumers. While the advertising industry itself does not entirely fall under the fitness category, it is certainly included in it and plays a major role in the success or failure of fitness companies.

The fitness industry is considered to include both fitness centres such as gyms as well as weight loss centres. Here we are concerned with the fitness side - businesses that primarily provide infrastructure such as space, equipment, and training in exchange for a membership fee. Gyms used to be big box stores - lots of equipment for cardio and weight training, with personal training available, racquetball maybe, and a pool. And those are still around - but this is an industry that has seen variety become the spice of life. Traditional exercises are being transformed into specialties and new programs are being developed at a breakneck pace.

Science and medicine are going shoulder to shoulder with fitness and the study of human body and performance. The goal has become to promote a healthy active lifestyle rather than just saving lives. It is an exciting phase for the fitness industry band absolutely anybody can become anything and it is passion that drives this industry forward.

The fitness industry is one of the biggest industry spanning out in all sectors of economy and business. The fitness industry is primary made up of service sector manufacturing sector and Wellness sector. There is retailing wholesale and distribution of fitness equipments and supplements along with its manufacturing even the advertising and marketing sector benefits immensely from the fitness industry. Fitness first started as a discipline then for recreation well-being to now as a way of life. Fitness industry has grown so huge that it has undertaken a lot of other business sectors under its umbrella and is ever spreading into the existence of human life. Fitness has become a Lifestyle. Fitness industry is worth over 80 billion USD globally, that is, the global industry is worth over 5.5 lakh crores of Rupees globally and the Indian Fitness Industry itself is worth over 14 billion Dollars, that is, over 95,500 crore rupees and is ever expanding and increasing. The wellness market in India registered a growth rate of 18-20% during 2012. The Government of India has recognized "wellness" as a priority sector in the "Make in India" campaign which shows that the Government does recognize the fitness industry of prime importance. India is having a population of over 1.3 billion people and fitness being an essential part of life, existence and well being, the need to cater to this demand is of prime importance and along with "Make in India" the government of India had also been promoting sports under "Khelo India". Sports and fitness go hand in hand, but it is not just sports and wellness but also health, fitness, well-being and a holistic approach to life. The fitness industry is at the center of quality of life. Now speaking about our Indian Population which being over 130 crores of people, the reach of fitness industry is only 0.5-1% of the total population that means about 65 lakhs to 13 crores of people go to a gym and over 128 crores of people are not into exercising or in the gym. The average age of an Indian will be 29 years of age by the year 2020. Over 70% of the population is above the age of 14 years while only 5% of the population is above 65 years of age. That means over 90 crores of Indians should be working out in the gym or playing a sport. Sports and fitness go hand in hand as any sportsman has to be fit in order to perform better and sports science has pushed sporting performance to the next level and every sport has become super competitive and records are being broken and made on a regular basis. Any sportsman who slacks with fitness or ignores the fitness routine or physical training ends up compromising with his/her performance and results. Fitness is not just related to physical well being and excelling in sports but it is essential to excel in any career of your choosing or calling. A fit and a healthy body means a healthy mind.

Fitness Industry - manufacturing, agriculture, service sector, wholesale, retail, distribution, marketing and advertising, apparels and accessories, real estate, franchising, branding, education, recreation, entertainment, show business, publishing, medical and healthcare, software application developer, e-commerce, counselling, science and research. The fitness industry is ever expanding and is a happening place to be not just for personal well being but as a career. Even today a personal trainer is not that respected as a lawyer, doctor, consultant, businessman or anything as such although his/her clients do have a certain kind of respect and trust in his/her trainer. A knowledge backed trainer with a keen interest in doing his/her own study and research is the best fitness professional or any professional that one can find. There are so many sectors within the fitness industry and one can start from any of this sector but the prime driver is the enthusiasm towards fitness and health which will take one forward. It is the passion that drives anything forward.

NUTRITION/SUPPLEMENTATION

Nutrition has always been considered of importance since the time when man wore grass skirts and went for hunting.

Legend has it that in Ancient Greece during the 6[th]century, a wrestler paid prime attention to his diet and training and he used to eat 9kgs of meat and 9kgs of bread and drank 20 bottles of wine daily to become big and strong. So the giant basically consumed over 57,000 calories daily, that is a lot of food and this legend is difficult to digest mentally but then who knows he might have consumed that much daily as today's strongman easily consume over 3kgs of meat daily. That is a lot of food.

Food is what gives us energy and nutrition. The food we eat makes up what we are and our performance is totally based on Nutrition. One simply cannot expect muscles to grow without eating food.

In the fitness industry and also in sports science, nutrition is of prime importance and is popularly recognized as Sports Nutrition. Also called as Exercise Nutrition.

Exercise Nutrition is the role of food and nutrition to perform better at an exercise or a physical activity. It may be moving faster or lifting heavier or to perform for longer duration. So basically nutrition is targeted either for endurance or for strength.

Most of the initial studies have been on metabolism of Carbohydrates and fats. Carbohydrates convert into glycogen stores which are the energy reserves while fats are stored energy used by an athlete for performances.

The studies on protein have still been difficult as protein is present all over the body and research on protein is still going on as to how protein synthesis happens and how protein plays a major role in our body. Muscles are made up of protein and have glycogen storage in them. So we can say that the studies on Carbohydrates and fats have been simpler while studies on protein are complex comparatively.

Carbohydrates play a major role in an athlete in a sporting event as glycogen stores are used up at a faster rate in a sporting event. A marathon runner or an endurance athlete should consume more or less 9 grams of Carbohydrates per kilo of body weight, so basically a 60kg athlete needs to consume 60*9 = 540gms of Carbohydrates daily during training periods, that is 50-60gms of Carbohydrates per hour to maintain blood glucose levels.

In sporting history, as per nutrition, the weirdest and a funny one about nutrition story is that of marathon runners. The early marathon runners in the early 1900's did and ate all it took to finish their marathon race be it stealing peaches from a car or begging for apples at an orchard or fuelling up on rat poison. Even alcohol played a major role and the ever favourite being egg whites. Things are not so now and have improved incredibly in the field of sports nutrition.

Many sports have tried to include alcohol and beer in their training but if we look at it closely it is nothing but providing instant calories to the body after training and then some alcohol is also fruit based and also numb the mind to the fatigue that sets in after training. Alcohol is a big no when it comes to a healthy lifestyle and for performance.

Eugen Sandow and then another bodybuilder Earle Liederman advocated the use of beef extract or beef juice as a supplement to enhance muscularity.

The first sports drink is said to be Gatorade developed by Dr. Robert Cade for a university team Gators in America. It is basically a Carbohydrates/glucose drink which is available in the market and is one of the most successful sports drink. Gatorade was developed in 1965.

In 1930, whey was processed from milk. This method of processing whey from milk which is fit for human consumption was developed by pharmacist Eugene Schiff. His company Schiff Bio foods sold whey to local drug stores.

Before whey being used, the protein supplements were soy based which are still available in the market.

The supplement industry is worth over 37 billion dollars as of 2015 reports.

Meanwhile the Indian supplement industry is hardly worth a billion dollars. The major draw back being that hardly 1% of the population is into fitness, so the awareness of good nutrition is lacking. The traditional based food diets as well as regionally influenced food does not let food and nutrition awareness possible. Spreading awareness about nutrition does not mean promoting western food habits but to be able to inculcate sports nutrition into the Indian food habits by using traditional or regional foods quantitatively as well as qualitatively.

The saddest thing in the Indian supplement market is our own attitude and zero inclination towards Indian supplement brands and our preference to import whey rather than processing it here when we have such a huge dairy industry.

Even if AMUL concentrates on production of whey - we can be the number one whey manufacturer in the world but then we are put down by corruption and government bodies who are least interested in research and development and are only inclined towards minting money.

The Indian Dairy Industry is worth over 40 billion dollars but there is no whey.

As a consumer we are also interested only in foreign brands and even some trainers and nutritionist openly advocate that Indian brands cannot be trusted nor its manufacturing in India. We ourselves accept and advocate that foreign brands are the right way to whey.

Most of the Indian brands prefer importing raw whey from foreign countries and flavouring/mixing them in India as it is cheaper and the quality of whey is assured.

The Indian Supplement industry has a long way to go and needs to focus on manufacturing and branding.

Although there is a lot of innovation as to providing healthy foods and packet meals, the reach of such products and services is very limited like operating in only one city. India is a huge market because of the population and this population needs to be well fed and for this awareness is required.

The supplement industry also provides athletes with sponsorships and are very good marketing platforms for the fitness industry.

FITNESS ACADEMIES/ TRAINING/ COACHING CENTRES.

In India there is a need of having qualified knowledgeable fitness trainers and Nutritionists to make India a fit and healthy nation.

Fitness Science is ever expanding and there is a continuous research and studies being conducted on human performance.

In Bodybuilding it has basically started by trial and error methods and this approach is still very effective in Bodybuilding. It has been termed as bro science and although it has been ridiculed many a times but bro science does actually make sense but then any experiment does make sense be it a positive or negative result.

In fitness science only knowledge is not effective but knowledge with experience goes a long way. Self-Study and research is the way to go forward if one wants to succeed in the fitness industry.

ONLINE TRAINING

Now as we have seen that training programs were mail ordered but since the advent of the internet and the world wide web, training programs are online through e-mail, WhatsApp, Skype, Instagram, websites, apps and any other Internet based communication application. Many trainers have promoted themselves and given training online since the 1990'a and now any person with a Six pack calls himself to be a personal trainer or coach and the knowledge they spread can be anything from genuine to utter bogus crap. Any kind of fluctuations in food habits or exercise regime is going to give a result but is it healthy or beneficial in the long run is a question which matters the most but is neglected the utmost. Every fitness program is a tailor made program for the individual, you simply cannot copy paste the same program to everyone else and expect the same results.

FITNESS INDUSTRY - Beyond weight training and return - an infinite loop.

Now when we look at fitness industry, we primarily look or focus onto a gym and weight training. With the awareness of fitness and the need for a physical activity for health and well-being as an integral part of life, many forms and arts have merged into the universe of fitness industry. Every physical activity is studied and being promoted as an activity of fitness, health and well-being. Fitness is a necessity but this necessity should be fulfilled by a way which makes it fun and entertaining. Fun and entertainment is a personal perspective. Fitness and health are objective but the method to be fit and healthy is subjective.

Objective is a perception devoid of emotions/opinions or personal feelings and is based upon fact which is quantifiable and can be measured.

Subjective is a perception purely based upon the emotional condition of the person based upon personal opinion/inclination.

Objective approach is far better than a subjective one because change takes place when objectivity is applied upon the subjective.

We as fitness professionals have to make sure that people are into a physical activity for fitness, health and well-being. So we need to understand what each activity will do for the body and mind and how it will benefit and create awareness for overall well-being of mankind.

So many roads to fitness and well-being but as studies show and the way things are moving forward - weight training is and has to be the essential activity of fitness and performance.

Many sportsmen and coaches are inculcating weight training in their training regimen in order to excel in their field and improve their performance. Even doctors are advocating weight training for health and well-being and studying something as simple as muscle contraction and how weight training benefits the human body.

So any fitness regime is going to be incomplete without weight training or resistance training.

CAREERS IN THE FITNESS INDUSTRY

The golden rule to be a part of this huge industry is - "Practice before you preach and research till you breathe."

Now as we have gone through this whole introduction and history and time capsule of the fitness industry, you might have got an idea that there is a lot to do in order to make a living in the Fitness Industry and to be successful. Career on the gym floor as a trainer or at the desk, organising competitions and events, manufacturing, retailing, distributorship, apparels, design, education and research, sales, entrepreneur and so on

There is a lot to do in the fitness industry and one can pursue one's passion in any way forward in the fitness industry. People not having knowledge about fitness and health tend to look questionably when you tell that you are a trainer. The respect and love that a trainer gets for the services is only known by the instructor and instructee as a trainer is more of a mentor than just a trainer and a guide who looks after the well-being of the member/client. Many of us start out as trainers ending owning our own gym or a studio but the key to success and progress is research and innovation.

There are many hurdles in the fitness industry and creating awareness is of utmost importance. There is a need to change the mind-set of the people - it is easy to stay alive and live our your life but it's important to lead a healthy life. As we age we deteriorate faster and start looking older for their age or have one or the other physical ailments or dis - ease. Gyms can be found empty but hospitals and clinics are houseful like a block buster movie being released one after the other.

Science and medicine are going shoulder to shoulder with fitness and the study of human body and performance. The goal has become to promote a healthy active lifestyle rather than just saving lives. It is an exciting phase for the fitness industry band absolutely anybody can become anything and it is passion that drives this industry forward. It does not really matter how qualified you are education wise but if you have thirst for knowledge and excellence then fitness industry will lead you to your success.

Market Research by Raj Lanjekar –

India is developing at a fast clip and competitive lifestyle has led to increased stress levels. Anxiety, depression, high blood pressure, and lack of sleep are common even among the Gen X and this has given way to the rise of the wellness industry.

According to a study by McKinsey & Company the wellness industry is currently valued at $1.5 trillion globally. This study analysing 7,500 consumers in 6 countries (including India) has offered key insights into consumer behaviour. The consumer trends in this study can be grouped into the following broad categories: -

HEALTH: People are investing in many remote medical devices that can constantly monitor their state of well-being. With the increase in popularity in digital wearables, telemedicine, and remote patient monitoring services, this trend is bound to increase.

NUTRITION: Dieting has always been a significant part of being healthy. An increase in dietary food, supplements, and nutrition coaches has been observed in recent years.

FITNESS: People are exercising more whether it's jogging, going to the gym, investing in a Pedometer etc.

MINDFULLNESS: Introspection, understanding the body and its processes to the molecular level, and figuring out ways to implement clarity of thought and methods for improving focus have been huge draws for the wellness industry. Further, with central government's schemes like AYUSH and the introduction of International Yoga Day by the United Nations, this particular trend has seen enormous growth.

CHANGING TRENDS OF THE INDIAN WELLNESS INDUSTRY

Spurt in Organic Products: India has become one of the largest producers of organic products. A growing number of people are actively investing monthly in organically grown produce, organically processed meat, wood-pressed or cold-pressed oil, cosmetics made from organic materials, and clothes made from pure cotton instead of manufactured materials. People becoming more conscious of what they put in their bodies has led to a steady increase in organic shops across India.

Healthcare goes Phyigital: Apart from physical chemist stores, there has been an increase in popularity of telemedicine and remote-patient monitoring. Consequently, healthcare and the wellness industry are gaining an increased online presence. There is a plethora of online exercise videos, fitness and meditation apps which have flooded the internet space.

Increased Physical Activity and Nutritional Supplements: From using simple calcium supplements and energy drinks to adhering to a strict diet regimen, today's consumers are genuinely worried about falling sick, which has led to an increase in purchasing supplements.

Consumers have started buying Vitamin, Zinc, and Iron tablets to whip up their immunity. Indians have also begun consuming Gluten free cereals, cold-pressed juices, Avocados, and other food products recommended to be healthier alternatives.

Voice of Social Media Influencers: With the increase in online dependence, the voice of social media influencers is soon to be gospel when it comes to maintaining a fit body and healthy mind. Much like how mainstream celebrities endorse various products, the wellness industry has seen great rewards in deploying online influencers to support their products.

India has become a wellness hub globally with a 12 per cent growth per annum. The Make in India thrust will bring in more investments in this sector. The government has earmarked a budget of around Rs 3,400 crore for the next 5 years to set up and strengthen Ayush Wellness Centres under the National Ayush Mission. This has sparked a rise in start-ups in the wellness sector.

Undoubtedly, the global pandemic has given rise to a new consumer behaviour where they are becoming more conscious about their well-being and choosing a lifestyle which is sustainable and healthy.

The aftermath of the pandemic has resulted in increased implementation of technology, and with the acceptance in the consumer market in India, the wellness industry will evolve and grow further.

Home gyms: According to a recent poll of 2,000 people by OnePoll, 75% of people believe it's easier to stay fit at home. Since the COVID-19 pandemic began in early 2020,

64% of respondents stated that they're more interested in at-home exercise than ever before. As the uncertainty of the pandemic continues, it's anticipated that most people will stick with at-home workouts, dedicating living space to personalized home gyms. Notably, you can get in a good workout without needing to buy expensive equipment. The average American spent $95.79 on home gym equipment during quarantine considerably less than a gym membership. With a pair of dumbbells and exercise bands, you can make getting in shape accessible and affordable.

Apps for minimal-equipment exercise: Though using a home gym works for some people, many don't have enough space. What's more, it's possible to get in a good workout without spending a penny. Going forward, expect to see more people utilizing free YouTube videos and exercise apps to guide them through workouts. Many of these exercises require minimal or no equipment and use your body weight for resistance.

Post Covid Fitness Industry

The Covid Lockdown was the worst for the fitness and gym industry which led to many gyms being shut down because of the losses sustained and the exit of many prime players of the industry closing operations across India. Most trainers were left without a job and had to shift careers. Price wars for sustaining operations led to reducing membership fees while the demand of personal trainings grew at an exponential rate in the first phase and has now settled down to gyms taking less percentage of the personal trainings and increase membership fees to keep cash flows intact and holding on to management dominance. (gyms require huge investments and management has to generate the revenue to maintain the business, personal trainers are a part of the business but not the sole revenue source)

Footfalls in gyms have reduced because of the priorities and reduced purchasing power of the masses while the well to do have understood the importance of fitness and health, and have taken personal trainers to take care of the same for them.

Fitness, Health, Exercise, Nutrition and Wellness have become the new investments of the well to do as they understand that the age old saying of "health is wealth" is true to its core and makes sense u because what is the point of making money if you are not fit and healthy to enjoy the earnings. Hospitalization and healthcare is far more expensive and a major expense while fitness and health is an investment which makes life better giving dividends in the form of well-being and improving work efficiency. The essence of a quality life lies in health and mental well-being which can be achieved by long term investment in exercise, nutrition and wellness.

CHAPTER THREE

EXERCISE IS LIFE SKILL

Definition of Life Skill – a skill that is necessary or desirable for full participation in everyday life.

Life skills are defined as "a group of psychosocial competencies and interpersonal skills that help people make informed decisions, solve problems, think critically and creatively, build healthy relationships, empathize with others, and cope with and manage their lives in a healthy and productive manner." According to the World Health Organization (WHO).

The WHO definition ends with the terms health and productive. For good health, exercise is a must and with health being in optimum state, an individual can be productive in life. Exercise engages both the mind and body and keeps the regenerative process of the body active while making us self-aware. Studies have shown that exercise alleviates stress and stress symptoms and release the hormones essential for feeling good and sense of accomplishment – be it running 5 miles or lifting a personal best gives that sense of confidence that is carried forward in all aspects of life.

The idea that Exercise is a life skill came to my mind when one of my closest friend was leaving for her further studies to Canada and that for the first time in her life she was going to be alone away from the love and care of her family and would have to look after her own nutrition and well-being. She is a good person and adapts well with everyone as being caring and a wonderful human being but then everybody is prone to being home sick and bouts of mild depression when being far from loved ones and in such a situation the one thing that I know for sure will help her is Exercising as it will release the feel good hormones and make her stronger and more confident towards her endeavours.

Those who work out in gyms and are persistent know that gym feels like home and it is where you meet yourself and focus on self-improvement. People walk away from the gyms or do not join ever because of misconceptions and the lack of guidance. Building a physique is not as easy as being fit and that is why people lose the interest or do not join at all. Your mind, your muscles and you all need to work in tandem to make it happen.

The basic necessities of life are food, clothing, shelter, education, access to the internet and the knowledge of exercise as all this will give a holistic approach to life. Exercise includes not just movement but also peace of mind like Tai Chi which is movement in peace.

"It is a disgrace to grow old through sheer carelessness before seeing what manner of man/woman you may become by developing your bodily strength and beauty to their highest limit. But you cannot see that, if you are careless; for it will not come of its own accord." - Socrates

MENTAL HEALTH BENEFITS OF EXERCISE

1. Reduces stress.

2. Healthy body is a healthy mind. If the body is healthy and active, then there is a less chance of falling sick.

3. Feel good factor.

4. Counters depression.

5. Improves self-confidence.

6. Prevents cognitive decline - keeps the brain functioning effectively and efficiently.

7. Alleviates anxiety.

8. Boosts brainpower - co-ordinated and focused movements improve brain function and concentration.

9. Sharpens the memory.

10. Helps control addictions.

11. Increases relaxation.

12. More energy leads to active life.

13. Boosts creativity.

14. Improves sleep.

Physical exercise prepares you to deal with any phase of life and working out in the gym makes you more focused and learn life lessons to tackle any situation. Training not only makes your body strong but also makes your mind stronger. Training imparts discipline and dedication which can be and is helpful in career and life. Training changes the mind-set of the individual making him/her more focused in life. There is an abundance of energy flow created by physical exercise and this energy can be channelled into all spheres of life and improves his/her quality of life.

CHAPTER FOUR

HOW TO TRAIN?

How to Train?

- What is exercise?
- Why to exercise?
- How to exercise?
- How to make training engaging?

Emotional Connect

Mental Connect

Mind Body Awareness

Sense of Strength and Purpose

Competitive and Progressive

Fun and Full filing

Awaken the superhero within you – superman, goku, wonder woman, what not inside of you.

What is Exercise?

Definition of Exercise -

"Exercise is any bodily activity that enhances or maintains physical fitness."

Dictionary meaning of Exercise -

noun

Activity requiring physical effort, carried out to sustain or improve health and fitness.

verb

Engage in physical activity to sustain or improve health and fitness.

Example - Bob exercised every day to stay healthy.

Now from the above definition and dictionary meaning it is clear that exercise is about performing a physical activity with the intention of improving health.

I drink tea every morning, my hand lifts the cup and gets it to my mouth and then I sip on the tea and keep the cup down, now this is a physical activity and I do it every day on daily basis. Does this improve my health? Tea is good, it's refreshing. That definitely improves my health. But then can drinking tea be considered as exercising? The answer is no.

Does going to the gym daily or for a walk amount to exercise? Does going for playing a sport just for the sake of playing amount to exercising? Answer is still "NO".

The word "exert" has a relation with the word exercise. Exert means to make a rigorous effort, which again means a thorough and a careful effort. Hence we can say that where the word "exercise" is used then it should be a rigorous effort towards improving health and fitness. It should be an activity which challenges the body and an actual effort is being made to perform that activity. It should not be as easy as a walk in the park. Exercise to exert, to challenge yourself to feel truly active than mere existence.

"Exercise is a physical activity carried out thoroughly and carefully to CHALLENGE the mind and the body in order to improve the individual's base levels of mind and body conditioning. It is a habitual activity to maintain optimum levels of fitness by targeting all the 5 components of fitness."

5 components of fitness are - Cardio - respiratory endurance, muscular endurance, muscular strength, ·flexibility and body composition all need to be at good levels to lead a good life.

There are 4 main types/categories of exercises based upon the types of muscles that are utilized as well as the duration of utilization of the muscles and its actions. The 4 main types are -

1. Aerobic exercise.

2. Anaerobic exercise.

3. Flexibility.

4. Balance.

Why to Exercise?

Exercise basically helps us to keep our body and mind healthy. Do we know our body and mind are healthy? How can we tell we are healthy? General assumption or the one answer that comes to everyone's mind is that I am fine, could be better; I am thin so I am healthy; I am fat but I am fine; and so on. We do not really think much about our health till something starts going really wrong with it. Living is easy as you seem to be alive but a quality life comes only when you are physically and mentally active.

Most of the diseases from the viruses and bacteria and what nots have been taken care of my vaccines and other medical drugs and cures are available but with the advent of modern medical science and technological developments, the fad has changed to acquiring lifestyle diseases. Lifestyle diseases are nothing but the dis-ease caused by leading a sedentary lifestyle with indulgence and our very dear stress and inability to cope up with life situations be it personal or career oriented. We have anxiety and mild depression as we are more engaged in consuming unnecessary data rather than doing physical and active stuff.

Before the 20th century, people died mostly of diseases caused by an unknown virus or bacteria, but now we die more because of lifestyle diseases be it hereditary or self-acquired. About 1.5 million people die of diabetes each year and cardiovascular diseases take an estimated 17.9 million lives each year. Thyroid or PCOD might not kill you but a high level of cholesterol will, the previous make life a bit miserable and brings in additional health problems and they all start with screwing up your metabolism. People did physical labour before the 20th century and that required movement, the stone age man did not have food delivery apps, he had to go out and hunt or gather, later do farming and animal husbandry. The quality or nutrition of foods we grow is going down, the gap between rich and poor is ever increasing, imbalance in development of regions leads to lack of awareness and availability of resources is scarce. The problems are aplenty but then exercise only requires you and for you to move. Internet accessibility has reached everywhere and that should make awareness and knowledge exchange easy.

Our body is made up of muscles which are designed for movement and without movement we lose muscle mass as muscles are metabolically active and consume calories. The way most of us work now a day is sit at a desk and type so we might as well have been trees while our twigs did the typing and stuff. We made progress because we kept moving and performing actions and not because we sat and stared at a wall. The astronomers back then did stare at the night sky and were able make a map of celestial things and then have others build something out of it like the pyramids, they did not wait for somebody to give them the data so that they could code it and present it on a device.

They did both the physical and mental work.

Now you sit over there for 8 to 10 hours and do your work and then you spend time doing recreational activities sitting or lying down; get up and move.

How to Exercise?

Why the Gym is the best place to Exercise?

1. Gym is mostly an indoor activity so the outside weather conditions do not stop you from exercising.

2. Availability of various equipment to work on your overall health.

3. Exercises in the gym are easy and not at all complicated as they work the natural movements of the body.

4. Controlled and variable intensity of exercise within the available time frame which means you can have an effective workout session even on days when you are in a hurry.

5. Progressive growth in health and strength.

6. Better mind- body co-ordination and awareness.

7. The atmosphere in the gym motivates you to exercise. Celebs have said that if you are feeling like skipping on your workout just makes it to the gym and you will get motivated to workout.

8. Gyms have trainers who have a wide knowledge about health and fitness and can guide you as well as answer your questions regarding the same.

9. Gyms are a place where various people come and everyone having the same motive tend to help each other. Socializing is a part but do not make it the sole reason.

10. Injuries can be fixed in the gym. Rehabilitation after an accident or injury is done in a gym.

GYM SECTIONS

A. FREE WEIGHT SECTION

This consists of dumbbells, weight plates, barbells, rods, kettlebells, benches, mats, medicine balls, Swiss balls and wrist and ankle weights.

B. WEIGHT MACHINES SECTION

This section consists of all the exercise machines for weight training where the movements are specific and assisted.

C. CARDIO SECTION

This section is where cardio exercises are done with the use of machines like treadmills, elliptical trainer, exercycle, etc.

D. WEIGHT LIFTING SECTION

here is a dedicated space for lifting weights where compound and olympic lifts are practiced.

E. FLOOR EXERCISES SECTION

In this section body weight exercises, warm up drills and stretching is done.

Many a times the space allocated for Weight Lifting and floor exercises is the open space on the gym floor so be cooperative with your fellow gym members and exercise with care.

BENEFITS OF WEIGHT LIFTING
1. Very Effective for Fat Loss.
2. Weight Gain by increase in muscles.
3. Good personality.
4. Anti-ageing.
5. Increases bone density counters osteoporosis.
6. Stronger muscles protect joints.
7. Higher metabolism- burn more calories.
8. Releases endorphins - feel good hormones.
9. Improved concentration and focus.
10. Self-Awareness and co-ordination.

These are few of the benefits of weight lifting and it benefits males and females in equal amounts.

Girls please note that you are not going to get as muscular as boys as God has made you different in a beautiful and elegant way and weight lifting enhances these traits. Muscularity and masculinity is dependent on the male hormone testosterone which is very low in females while estrogen hormone is the female hormone which gives the softness.

How should your workout be?

1. Start with mobility drills/ warm up exercises.

2. Do bodyweight exercises like pushups, pull ups and bodyweight squats.

3. Do weightlifting exercises with dumbbells, bars and machines.

4. Do ab-crunches.

5. Do cardio (optional or have a whole day for cardio depending upon your goals.)

6. Stretching exercises.

An ideal workout is between 45-60minutes. Finish your workout within an hour to get the best result as the intensity of the workout matters more than doing multiple numbers of exercises.

Gym is not the only place for exercise, you can exercise wherever you are, be it at home or the office or on a vacation. Movement is the key. There are many exercise and training methods and you can adopt any that you like and enjoy doing, just do not do it mindlessly but try to understand and know why you are doing something and how it is benefiting you and your health. Playing sports is good but if you are not playing professionally but as recreation then adding a training and exercise regime is very important. Even if you go for walking or jogging or running, there needs to be a regime of mobility exercises, strength exercises and stretching. Exercise regime should target all the components of fitness.

How to make training engaging?

Training has to be structured and goal oriented with many milestones in between and the path and trajectory of development and progress can be measurable. It is a long continuous process and with every milestone or goal the approach has to change. It is all about getting better, stronger and fitter and also about maintaining optimum levels of health and fitness.

Emotional Connect – Man is an emotional creature and is driven more by emotions than logic. You tell a man that lifting weights is good for your health and that will not interest him much but if you tell him that lifting weights will make you look more good and more attractive, then ye he will be interested, even she will be interested. You tell a diabetic that exercising will help him to control his sugar levels it might not interest him but if you tell it will help him enjoy food and have a bit of his favourite sweet, bang on "dil ko chuh liya yaar" words straight to the heart.

Emotional connect herein I mean to say that while exercising you can let out your frustrations and stress which are all emotional aspects and channelize the energy to becoming a better version of you.

Mental Connect – Exercise requires you to be aware of your won movement and fire the right neurons to make the movement possible. One simply cannot perform an exercise mindlessly unless and until you become a master at it and have performed the same movement in practice a million times. Lifting that dumbbell makes your brain aware as to the load in your hands and then engages the required muscles to enact the required movement.

Mindless movements do not bring results and if that ever did then you would have had bulging biceps just from sipping tea.

Mind Body Awareness – With mental connect you develop mind body awareness which is a domain of athletes of pay at professional levels. All of us will not be professional athletes but all of us need to develop this skill which will help us to avoid injuries and pains in day to day activities. This skill so developed through exercising also makes us more aware of moods and manage stress and cope up with whatever life throws at you be it in your career or your life. The Mindfulness Program of The Human Excellence Network focuses on developing the same in every individual.

Sense of Strength and Purpose – When you break the barriers of your physical performance, your mind becomes stronger to deal with the barriers and roadblocks in your professional and personal life. The Can Do Attitude is developed through exercising.

Competitive and Progressive –The Can Do Attitude developed through exercising helps you to develop a competitive and progressive approach towards all aspects of life with a positive approach.

Fun and Full filing – The more you find yourself through exercising, the more fun you have doing it and find it full filing and the same approach is applied towards all aspects of life.

Awaken the superhero within you – superman, goku, wonder woman, what not inside of you – all aspects of life. Our heroes are our source of inspiration and you can be your own hero and not just inspire your own self but even those around you.

All these apects and approaches can be used by a Fitness Trainer as well as an individual who wants to lead a healthy lifestyle and begin his/her journey towards fitness and health.

CHAPTER FIVE

FOUNDATIONS OF THE MASTER TRAINER

– Foundations of the Master Trainer

- Who is a Trainer?
- Who is your Master Trainer? You are your own trainer. A teacher is always a student.
- You can open yourself to learn and when you are truly a student the universe is your master and along your journey you will meet many teachers in the form of humans, books, technology and so on. Awareness is the key.
- A mentor is not just teaching the mentee but is also learning how to train the mentee while imparting knowledge and technical knowhow of things.
- SelfReflection and Self Realization.

- Know thyself – biomechanics and mind muscle connection.

Introduction

Anybody can become a trainer and the way the fitness industry has been going for past few decades, absolutely anyone becomes a trainer, being knowledgeable and experienced is not the list when it comes to hiring or becoming a trainer – what is required is the will to work at low wage and should have the passion or interest in exercising at the gym. Even I have hired absolute no brainers who just wanted a job and had no qualification to be anything other than a trainer (did train them to handle the floor and know how to perform exercises).

The reason for the selection criteria for a trainer's job is so weak and poor with lack of qualifications is because the public at large does not prioritize exercise and fitness as an essential part of their life. "You are treated the same way you value or treat others."

In 2003, I used to pay 500 Rupees for a monthly gym membership, and when I opened my first gym back in 2016, I collected 500 Rupees monthly gym membership from customers (I primarily focus on hard-core gyms with only weight training equipment) and, even now in 2022, if you take the annual gym membership at my gym, you average out at less than 500 rupees per month. All the prices, inflation and every other thing has increased by many a times but somehow gym memberships have remained the same and the reason being that people do not value or give importance to fitness and health.

Prices of everything else has increased, a loaf of bread was just 10 rupees back in 2003 which now costs 40 odd rupees in 2022. A bottle of beer was anywhere between 60 to 80 rupees in 2003, which now costs anything above 150 rupees, but price of gym is still 500 rupees starting and that too for whole month. One can argue that the number of gym establishments have increased in the vicinity but then data shows that less than 5% of the total population goes to a gym or has a gym membership. Exercise is needed by everyone, then where are the rest of the people?

Fitness and Health should be the priority of every individual and should come in the category of Life Necessities and Essential Needs/services. One simply cannot live life staying at home or office and by buying health insurance policies. Health insurance policies and medical bills keep increasing year on year and we wilfully pay for those without bargaining but while buying a gym membership we ask for discounts and what nots. You need to exercise and stay fit which is your primary defence against dis-ease and for quality of life, and quality of life should not be considered as cheap and of least importance.

"Nothing in life worth having comes cheap or easy."

Who is a trainer?

[Educational Slide by Veenita –

"A Trainer is an individual who provides knowledge and guidance through organized techniques subject to a specific field of expertise."

"A Personal Trainer is one who creates and delivers safe and effective exercise programs for apparently healthy individuals and groups, or those with medical clearance to exercise. (as per Wikipedia)]

A trainer is a knowledgeable person who has his/her own self-experience of exercising and training be it in the gym or any other organized physical activity and has himself practiced the movements and exercises that he/she wishes to teach or guide others in and knows how to perform those movements with least to none scope for injury. Other than knowledge and experience, the trainer needs to have people skills and soft skills to handle any person in the gym or outside and should be attentive, responsive and responsible person who is aware of bodily movements and mental toughness. The trainer who is observant is a good trainer as he/she can spot any slight short comings in the performance of the movements.

Role of a Personal Trainer -

Personal training is a fulfilling career, but you won't succeed unless you strive to improve every day. If you want to make your clients so happy that they will tell all their friends about you, check out these seven habits of highly successful personal trainers.

Approach towards Clients

One should be focused

What's the point of asking a young soccer mom to perform max lifts if her primary goal is fat loss? There isn't one, but a lot of personal trainers are guilty of projecting their own values onto their clients. Remove your ego from the equation. If an exercise doesn't meet your client's needs and goals, then it's a waste of time.

We are human too

Personal trainers should care about their health, but that doesn't mean they have to eat steamed broccoli every day. Everyone has a guilty pleasure or two, Share little details like this with your clients. It's important for them to understand that the occasional indulgence won't hurt them as long as they make healthy decisions most of the time.

Preach what you practice

If a mother tried to convince her children to stop eating so much sugar with a can of Coca-Cola in her hand, how effective do you think she would be? Not very! Those kids would laugh her out of the room! Don't expect people to take you very seriously if you don't follow your own advice. I'm not saying you have to be perfect, but you'll have an easier time finding clients if you walk the walk.

Clients ask questions

Resist the temptation to lecture your clients. If you've ever been to a boring college class, you know your clients won't retain much information from a lengthy lecture. Instead, let them do the talking. I like to ask my clients to tell me about a time they made an impulsive eating decision. This helps me determine the triggers that influence their behaviour. It also gives me the opportunity to ask them what they could do differently next time to make a better decision, which improves future compliance.

Educate your clients.

"If I give away too much advice, my clients might decide they don't need me anymore!" Sound familiar? Don't worry about it. If that was really the case, they wouldn't have hired you in the first place, because you can find all kinds of advice for free on the Internet. Explain things like anatomy, proper form and exercise selection as time goes on. Your clients might even share an interesting thing you said with a friend, which could result in a referral if you're lucky.

Don't use too much lingo (Technical words)

It might seem odd to mention this because I just told you to educate your clients, but hear me out. It's good to teach your clients, but you need to do so in a language they will actually understand. I know you can point out the latissimus dorsi on a diagram of the human body, but the average person can't even pronounce it. Just call them "lats" and make sure your client understands the important that they are the broadest muscle group on your back and should be activated during exercises like rows and chin-ups.

Provide homework assignments

Your clients don't live at the gym. Their lives can't revolve around fitness, because they have a lot of responsibilities. It's hard to find the time to prepare healthy meals when you're a single parent or a busy professional. You need to understand this struggle, because your clients' results depend on it. A little bit of exercise couldn't possibly make up for a whole lot of poor eating decisions. Give your clients some "extra credit" assignments they can do in between sessions.

For example, there's a book called "Fix, Freeze, Feast" that teaches people how to cook in bulk. It's a lot easier to prepare healthy meals when you can limit cooking to one day per week. If you have a client whose most common excuse is a lack of time, you ask them to read this book. Then, you ask them to pick out five to 10 recipes that sound healthy *and* tasty. If they have children, I ask them to involve the kids in this process (because they must be on-board with the idea for it to be sustainable!).

Identify the most common struggles of your clients. Find some books and articles that involve that subject to use as inspiration for your own homework assignments.

Customer Service excellence

First, knowing what it is and providing an experience, not a session. Give give give to the client during, after, before. Go the EXTRA mile. Preparing for a session? What you should do, not extra. Providing water and a towel- minimum expectation. Providing a stretch before they leave? nothing special. But a stretch, a photo illustrating it and instructions on a YouTube video in their inbox within the day after a session- that's getting there.

Appearance. You look too good, you intimidate your clients for the most part who need you most. You're selling personal training - hope- dreams- faith. You're preparing better parents, spouses, employees and bosses. Look like a professional personal trainer. Not a professional anything else. Shave, shower, smell clean not like a perfume counter.

Adapting

The personal trainer characteristics that help clients to succeed will include a willingness to assist and respond appropriately to client needs. Trainers must also be careful to oversee and communicate the principles of the training program in a manner that is safe to the client. When the training becomes difficult, or when the client lacks the necessary motivation to follow the program through areas of challenge; the personal trainer must be perceptive enough to know when to offer adequate support and encouragement.

Commitment

Being a personal trainer require commitment to the program that is designed to realize both a long term and short term set of goals. If the program is not going as expected, the trainer must restructure the program in order to suit the needs and ability of the client that they are training. It takes patience to deal with clients and to work in a sequential manner through the parameters of the designed program. Trainers must never become frustrated with their clients and must always strive to keep on track, and lead the client through the program despite difficult times.

Prepare and pay attention to details

Trainer often write the session as they go. They haven't thought about progression or what happened last time. They base the workout on how the client "feels"- how is that a lot different than what the client might have done themselves? When you do write a program, too often I see a plan look like "10x" or "3 x 12" without any indication of what weight. If I were the trainer forced to take over at the next session...I'd be in trouble. There are no notes or changes made to a workout plan....really? It never goes exactly like you planned it- things go slower or faster, you have to do a heavier or lighter weight based on the client's day and status. You have to do fewer repetitions or can do more than you planned. When there is no feedback written in the margins, I'm keenly aware that there isn't much "big picture" thinking going on there.

Future plans

A successful trainer is always thinking about what's next. He or she knows their niche, the kind of clients they attract is showing a pattern and they are thinking about the next group training, the next book, the next article or freelance piece they'll create...they are thinking about long term successful fuelled by finding a solution to a problem many people have.

Who is your Master Trainer? You are your own trainer. A teacher is always a student.

In the Fitness Industry, the designation of a Master Trainer is given to the one who has immense knowledge and the technical know-how of performing exercises and has the experience of training many clients over a considerable period of time and he who has himself practiced the proper form and technique a many times under strict observations.

"The master has failed more than the beginner has even tried."

Practice makes perfect, there is no place for perfection but only a place or scope for improvement. Perfection is the end but improvement is the journey of adaptation to changes.

Not every trainer can be a master trainer but every individual can become their own master trainer- the approach is self-awareness, self-reflection and self-realization.

By Veenita -

Self-reflection (also known as personal reflection) is taking the time to think about, meditate on, evaluate, and give serious thought to your behaviours, thoughts, attitudes, motivations, and desires. It's the process of diving deep into your thoughts and emotions and motivations and determining the great, "Why?" behind them.

Without self-reflection, we simply go through life without thinking, moving from one thing to the next without making time to evaluate whether things are actually going well. We don't pause to think, to analyse, to determine what is going well and what isn't working. The unfortunate result is that we often get stuck. For example, a lack of personal reflection may lead us to stay in a job we don't like or a relationship that isn't going well.

A lack of self-reflection causes us to simply keep running, trying to keep up with things even if things aren't going well. We feel like we're simply trying to keep our heads above water. We end up doing the same things over and over again, even if those things aren't producing the results we hoped for.

Self-realization – We all come with a USER MANUAL (mostly it is you who has access to it) How often are you distracted, lost in your thoughts, or overwhelmed by difficult emotions?

Being in the present is more difficult than ever with technology today. The bright side of the world is display on social media while some portray the little dark patches for the sake of sympathy. We are all becoming dopamine addicts and the source is not long lasting or effective but stuff brought from a shady drug dealer.

Self-awareness is about being true to your own self and the ability to observe and analyse your life from a third person perspective. When you are able to do this you are on the path of excellence.

"You can open yourself to learn and when you are truly a student the universe is your master and along your journey you will meet many teachers in the form of humans, books, technology and so on. Awareness is the key."

In order to be good at anything, one has to keep on upgrading his/her knowledge and learn new methods, books, research work, etc. and keep practicing his/her art as there is always a scope for improvement and no-one can truly become the master and know everything about a topic as every given moment there are new ideas and innovations. Even a trainer has to keep upgrading and acquiring new knowledge and skills in order to help his clients be fitter and stronger. Doing a certification or a diploma in the field of study of fitness science will only open you to a method of structured learning and help you in your further studies. Most of the courses on personal training and nutrition out there are basic knowledge and know-how and even some degree courses or undergraduate courses do not really touch the depths of the topics as they are vast and deep. We, at The Human Excellence Network are aiming to create courses in fitness science in a way to reach a certain depth that will make our students acquire knowledge which will help the society and make the fitness industry an authority when it comes to human health and performance.

The idea is to create a knowledge bank in the field of fitness science and curate the same, in order to make it easily accessible as well as easy to understand so that anybody can pick up the same and pursue a fruitful career in the fitness and healthcare industry and to promote research work in the same.

Knowledge grows when it is shared and there is an interaction and exchange of ideas and know-how which is why T.H.E.N is a network of knowledgeable and passionate people wanting to learn and know more about fitness sciences. The universe is our teacher and we only need to be aware and observant.

"A mentor is not just teaching the mentee but is also learning how to train the mentee while imparting knowledge and technical know-how of things."

Every individual is unique and different when it comes to learning, understanding and performing. This is something that every trainer/mentor should know and understand. Personal Training is not an easy task but involves a lot of emotional intelligence along with technical know-how of training and this needs to be understood by the client. The PT is not someone who just shows you what to do and to move your weights but someone who is trying to help you in a way which suits and caters to your individual character and attitude to make you perform better and get fitter and healthier. It is the client who is going to benefit the most out of the program while a knowledgeable and trained trainer will be using his skill sets and getting things done from you. You doing bicep curls is not going to make your trainer's bicep grow. It is one to one relationship which is beneficial for the client and a learning curve for the trainer.

BIOMECHANICS AND MIND MUSCLE CONNECTION

Definition of Biomechanics –

Biomechanics is the science of a living body, including how muscles, bones, tendons, and ligaments work together to produce movement.

Biomechanics, in science, is the study of biological systems, particularly their structure and function, using methods derived from mechanics, which is concerned with the effects that forces have on the motion of the bodies. Contemporary biomechanics is a multidisciplinary field that combines physical and engineering expertise with knowledge from the biological and medical sciences. There are multiple specialty areas in biomechanics, such as cardiovascular biomechanics, cell biomechanics, human movement biomechanics, occupational biomechanics, and sport biomechanics. (Encyclopedia Britannica)

MIND MUSCLE CONNECTION

What is the mind? Over here we will consider the mind to be both the brain which is inside your head and does all the processes of keeping you alive by sending signals and receiving inputs from inside the body and from outside of it, as well as that function of the brain which makes you think, learn, understand and implement. Hormones do play an important role in how the brain functions and as to how you think and react.

Muscles make movements possible at joints, without muscle there is no movement and it is the brain that sends the signal to the muscle to perform the movement/action. If the brain does not send the signal, then there is no movement. Movements are "response to stimuli" that means the movement is done on purpose or in need. Nothing is done without a purpose, strength is born out of necessity and not desire. Desire is a wishful thinking and a slight urge while necessity is essential. The body does not move without a reason unless you want it to move or the brain receives certain signals which demands movement like me shaking my leg right now while sitting and writing –

the mind is at unease with some other thoughts back in the (probably the mail that I did not sent/haven't sent) while I try to focus my attention to write these few paragraphs, the brain is trying to keep itself busy by sending signals to my leg so that I get distracted from the thoughts in the back of my head while I focus on writing. There is mind muscle connection and when you understand this relation you will be in better position of self-awareness.

The New Beginning

T.H.E.N is a network created to cater to the wellness requirements of our community and nation as a whole. Our mission is to bring awareness and transformation through products ranging from education in fitness science & nutrition, development of personal health through training programs, nutrition & counselling, to revolutionizing the industry with the ideas of sustainable living in a digital world.

Living in the epoch of a rat race, physical and mental well-being has become a topic of concern nowadays for those working in the corporate world. Desk jobs require your maximum time working in front of computers without any physical activity for hours.

Well, when this happens, your body starts showing signs of inactivity and fatigue. You won't have sufficient energy to do any work due to a lack of motivation. Especially in the remote working culture now. During the lockdown, there was a significant increase in BMI for youth and young adults (18-35 years) and physical activity decreased by 31.25%, for adults (36-65 years) by 26.05% and for the elderly (over 65 years) by 30.27%. There was a high level of Perceived Fragility and risk of getting infected for females and the elderly.

That said, we continue to observe patterns of similar inactivity even post-lockdown. Whether it's developing lifestyle disorders or mere habits that can lead to one.

We are here to impose the importance of Wellness at the workplace as well as at home and how to build the right habits to live a happy and stress-free life.

T.H.E.N APPROACH

Knowledge – Everybody else is trying to sell saying they are right and others are wrong when it comes to nutrition and training while all of them know that applied nutrition is not an exact science and varies from individual to individual when it comes to implementation. Most of the exercise models focus on gym exercises and creates variations to justify their authority. We step out of this smoke and mirror and deliver real knowledge and represent it as it is and teach how to apply the same. We create an in depth course/knowledge material and grade as per university standards and collaborate and have on board all professionals not just from sports and fitness fields but from the medical practitioners' field along with scientists dealing with the brain, biology and microbiology. First step is to get Skill India and International accreditation and go for the Education Board Recognition in order to become an authority in the field of fitness science.

Service – Counselling and Training Programs – Personalized approach addressing the real needs of the customer and providing solutions not just to improve health parameters but also improve overall wellbeing and performance. Provide health condition specific or therapeutic diets and training programs. Focus more on women health and wellbeing. How do we cater to our targeted audience? It is by first knowing and understanding the functioning of the body, hormones and thinking patterns or psychology. Multiple buyer personas to be identified. Habits and routines help us to identify buyer personas. This creates the need of presenting and delivering our service in variety and target specific rather than following a single format.

Every individual requires empathy, understanding and, a structure benefiting the individual's ecosystem which is his/her mind, body, heart and soul with an extended horizon encompassing personal and professional relationships and aspirations. The Human Excellence Network is the individual centric platform to help the said individual to bring out a better version by working on own self by the methods of self-exploration, self-realization and self-awareness.

Product A evolution – knowledge creation in both physical (print) and digital format and being taught, trained and researched in order to promote and impart real knowledge to bring about professionals to deliver an eco-system for human health and performance. From certification courses to diplomas to degrees and beyond. We teach to create thinkers and researchers and not just service providers. The developments in technology and software and artificial intelligence can help us create products or further develop those products which are already present in the market.

Service A evolution – developing the existing methods and systems of counselling, training and diagnosis which can evaluate the overall health of an individual/customer and provide sustainable solutions for good health and human performance.

Product B – Digital Platform (global)

Product C – App (global)

THE HUMAN EXCELLENCE NETWORK IS AN OPEN ENDED PLATFORM CREATED FOR COLLABORATING EXCELLENCE IN THE FIELD OF FITNESS SCIENCE, NUTRITION AND HEALTHCARE ALONG WITH PROVIDING AND USING THE DEVELOPMENTS IN ARTIFICIAL INTELLIGENCE AND TECHNOLOGY TO PROMOTE THE WELL BEING OF MAN IN HIS ENDEAVOURS OF HUMAN GROWTH AND PROGRESS.

The network is made up of a few individuals whose introduction is as follows -

NIKHIL MADUSKAR (Role at THEN: Cheif Operating Officer)

Nikhil is a resident fitness expert and founder of MindHACK NFSI. He is a certified personal trainer, nutritionist, sports psychologist, and philanthropist living in Pune, Maharashtra.

His mission is to cut through the noise in the health and fitness industry and to empower the community, especially women to create sustainable solutions for lasting health, happiness, and confidence. Nikhil holds a rich experience of over a decade in training, managing operations and business development for quite a few fitness associations in Pune.

Alongside devoting his life to Wellness, Nikhil was always intrigued to spread social awareness for women welfare &empowerment. He founded Daamini Foundation (2013 - 2022) to foster and conserve women rights. He was the Trustee/Director of Mahesh Foundation, Belgaum which was home to HIV+ children. While his social service maintained a valuable network of contributions in the community, he also leveraged his expertise in the fitness community by creating foundational knowledge through books like Basics of Gym &Fitness, Fitness Science &the Gym, Foundations of Fitness, Personal Trainer Course for Sciencebuilt, About Nutrition, Self-help Nutrition Kindle Ebook, and so on... which have been published during the years and available online for viewers.

With his diverse experience within the Fitness industry, Nikhil is now exploring his horizons to bring about a paradigm shift in the forces that determine and build careers in the Health &Wellness sector. His most recent initiative, THEN (The Human Excellence Network) contains some ground-breaking cultures that will revolutionize the wellness industry expectations infusing the mission, values, achievements, and personality development for all who want to step up and make a difference in this field.

Nikhils keen interest in contributing towards the growth, expansion and acceptance of Wellness in the society keeps him afloat to encourage young talents of our country. The Human Excellence Network will definitely conquer a substantial platform for the enthusiasts in the industry.

JOYSON JOEL (Role at THEN: Chief Training Officer)

Throughout his years of training clients from all walks of life, Joyson has motivated so many to stay on track and accomplish their fitness goals. He is an influential professional when it comes to training clients as well as projecting excellent guidance towards sports coaching, especially football.

Being a certified personal trainer and an athlete in football, Joyson has mastered the art of movement that helps in peak physical performance. Raised in Pune, Maharashtra, he has always been able to connect with the community here. This has resulted in his strong networking through the industry to bring forth innovative training techniques among his members for successful transformations.

Academically, Joyson studied MCA from Pune University and that meticulously adds to his initiatives in this industry to be more technologically sound and enabled.

He is layered with sports fitness since childhood and is also keen in reforming a guide towards women's health and fitness. Joysons role at THEN (The Human Excellence

Network) is crucial and will decode our vision to deliver an ecosystem that promotes health &performance.

He is already transforming lives through his brand Joel Fitness Den &his global initiative WeEvolve which will also comprise an online platform for coaching around the world.

VEENITA JOHNSON (Role at THEN: Director of Business Development and Communication)

Veenita is a firm believer that - movement should be an integral part of someones life. We are programmed to be active and not a slacker.

She has been actively contributing to the fitness industry for over a decade through her intensive training methods and novelty in bringing about a fitness revolution. HIIT&Run - the Burn Club, established in 2020 amidst the lockdown was one of her 1st few initiatives towards enabling people to CHOOSE a healthier lifestyle. The brands main objective is to ensure people always keep challenging their limits.

She has always been passionate about sports &fitness from a very young age. It has been a decade guiding people and also learning in the process. This is while still working full-time in corporate offices. Her extensive knowledge and experience in coaching professionals in Business Communication has driven her to consolidate that expertise with her passion to help the industry grow.

Veenita is a certified personal trainer and an expert in High Intensity Interval Training for the general population. Her workouts are tailor-made for everyone to support a healthy lifestyle.

In addition to this, she is a Wellness Consultant who counsels trainers to improve their communication skills and clients to build habits that help manage their lifestyle stress.

Veenita has participated in National Womens Bodybuilding &won the IFBB (International Federation of Bodybuilding) Womens Figure 2020 - Bronze for our country. This journey has taught her to have realistic and measurable goals to achieve based on preference &lifestyle.

Veenitas role at THEN will develop a shaping metamorphosis of a culture that will incorporate confidence &credibility for our future tribe in the industry.

Her ethos is that fitness should always be balanced with a persons lifestyle to remain sustainable. - Our gambit on this journey.

WELCOME TO THE HUMAN EXCELLENCE NETWORK